HELLO, HOLY SPIRIT

-DEVOTIONAL-

MICHAEL J. BEAN

Empowered Publications Inc.
Millry, Alabama

Empowered Publications Inc.
529 County Road 31
Millry, Alabama 36558

Cover Design by Briana M. Bean

All scripture references are taken from the
King James Version of the Bible.

Library of Congress Control Number:
2015933042
ISBN: 978-1-943033-21-8

Hello, Holy Spirit

- Devotional -

Michael J. Bean

This book is dedicated to my parents,
Joe and Juanita Bean.
Through their faithfulness to God,
a legacy has been left to me
of love for the Word of God,
and the work of the Holy Spirit.
For this, I will always be grateful.

Introduction

In remarkable fashion, Jesus became the Passover Lamb sacrificed for the sins of the World. (John 1:29) Several days following the Passover, an offering of First Fruits was to be offered to God. This is what we refer to on our calendar as Easter, and is fulfilled through the resurrection of Jesus who is the First Fruit of all believers who have died, but someday shall be resurrected. (I Cor. 15:23)

After the feast of Passover and the First Fruits, the symbolism continues through the celebration of Pentecost—a fifty day span. Passover was a mandated Jewish Feast so important that Jews from many countries attended the celebration. It also marked the beginning of the main harvest season. As part of the celebration, two loaves of bread were prepared, and waved to the Lord as a special offering. (Lev. 23:15-22) A beautiful symbol of the church composed of both Jews and Gentiles.

Within this setting the Holy Spirit was sent as a fulfillment of a promise previously given by the Lord. (Acts 1:4-5) When the Holy Spirit came, He filled those who had been waiting. They glorified God in the languages of those attending the Pentecost feast. (Acts 2:11) Immediately, the empowerment of the Spirit within them focused their attention on reaching the World with the message of Jesus Christ Savior and Lord.

The Holy Spirit was to the early church exactly what Jesus had promised. He became their Helper. (John 14:16) In a practical sense, the Holy Spirit helped the early church by miraculously opening doors for the gospel to be presented. He also gave words of warning and guidance when needed. He protected and provided during the severest of circumstances.

The goal of this study is for you to not only know about the Holy Spirit, but to know the Holy Spirit personally. He longs to be your friend and have communion with you every day. As you engage in this devotional, may you begin each session as if greeting your best friend by saying, "Hello, Holy Spirit."

Day 1

Listen
Matthew 11:15

Our culture has conditioned us to be either busy or rendered numb with entertainment. As a result, listening to God is—for the most part—non-existent for most believers. Many Christians would simply prefer someone tell them what God is saying. While it is important to have a pastor or spiritual leader listening to the gentle voice of the Chief Shepherd, the individual believer must also hear, and know the voice of the Holy Spirit.

It is easy to develop a listening ear to the voice of the Holy Spirit. The first step is to develop the discipline of setting aside a secret place, and a special time to meet with God. The best time for this is the first hours of the day. If God desires the first fruit of our increase, then surely He would desire to have the first hours of the day as well. (Isaiah 26:9; 50:4)

To hear the voice of the Holy Spirit, it is vital to develop a love for the Word of God. Jesus often referred to the Holy Spirit as the Spirit of Truth who would teach, guide, and bring cleansing to the believer. The Holy Spirit speaks through the Word of God. (John 14:26; 16:13)

It is also important to have a deep and abiding love for Jesus Christ. This relationship comes through the voice of the Holy Spirit as He reveals Christ's attributes and character. Then, God speaks into our lives to form us into the image of His Son, Jesus Christ (John 15:26).

Reflection: Make a commitment to spend time alone with God during your day. Ask the Holy Spirit to open the Word so you see Jesus like never before. Read your Bible. Start with the book of John.

Day 2

First Mention
Genesis 1:2

When we study the Bible, we can apply certain guidelines that will help us understand it better. One of those guidelines is called "first mention." This rule states that the first mention of a concept or principle in the Word of God holds special significance in how it is looked at, and interpreted throughout the rest of the Bible.

The first mention of the Holy Spirit in Scripture reveals an interesting insight. At the beginning of the creation process, we see Him "moving" (Genesis 1:2). Then, through the rest of Scripture, we see Him moving to accomplish the will of God (Romans 8:27). He moved on the family of Abraham, and brought them into the Promised Land. He moved on Mary, and Jesus came into the world. He moved on the early believers to form the church. The last mention of the Holy Spirit indicates He is still moving, and He invites us to move with Him (Rev. 22:17).

The Holy Spirit is constantly moving in our lives. His most important work for us as believers is to reveal and transform us to the image of Jesus Christ (Galatians 4:19). He will continue to do this work within us until Jesus's return (Philippians. 1:6).

However, just because the Holy Spirit is moving doesn't mean He is in a hurry. As God, He doesn't operate solely within the realms of time and space. Because He knows the beginning from the end, He does things with an eternal perspective. Don't lose faith in God to move in your life. He may not show up when you feel He should, but He is always on time.

Reflection: Take time today to look at Isaiah 40:13-26 and note the greatness of the Holy Spirit as God. Apply these verses to your life and praise God for His great power. Thank Him because He is concerned about your smallest difficulties. (vs. 27-31)

Day 3

Who is He?
John 14:26; 15:26

Volumes have been written about the person, and work of the Holy Spirit. Because the study of the Holy Spirit as God is so broad and multidimensional, it is easy to know about the Holy Spirit without knowing Him personally. While it is important to know—on an intellectual level—all we can about the Holy Spirit, we also should remember that knowing about the Holy Spirit doesn't necessarily mean that one is experiencing the life of the Spirit (2 Cor. 3:6).

This is especially true when a person seeks a relationship with the Holy Spirit based solely on the pursuit of blessings, gifts, and empowerment. While these gifts and empowerment are important, the most vital part of a believer's life is to know God. That is, to love the Lord with all our heart, soul, and mind (Matt. 22:37).

Jesus referred to the Holy Spirit as a person, introducing Him to the disciples as their personal Helper. Paul the Apostle went further, indicating the Holy Spirit has the elements of personality by showing the mind of the Spirit (Romans 8:27), the will of the Spirit (1 Cor. 12:11), and the emotion of the Spirit (Romans 15:30). Since the Holy Spirit is a person, we can know Him, and form a relationship with Him.

The Holy Spirit as a person can be more than a mere acquaintance to us. He can be our closest companion, with whom we have communion and fellowship (2 Cor. 13:14; Philippians. 2:1). This should be an important part of every believer's life. This means we must spend time with Him and gradually develop a relationship. This relationship should be so close that you and the Holy Spirit are best friends.

Reflection: We grow closer to God through the work of the Holy Spirit in our lives. Ask God to manifest Himself in you through the Holy Spirit.

Day 4

He is God!
Matthew 28:18-20

There is not enough space to begin writing about the Holy Spirit as God. The Holy Spirit is the third person of the Holy Trinity. This doesn't place Him lower than the Father and the Son. Rather, it separates Him as a person while making Him just as much God as the Father and the Son.

The Scriptures are filled with references to the Holy Spirit as deity. He was with the Father and Son, and equally involved with the creation of all things (Psalms33:6). He was part of the eternal counsel of God in determining Christ to be the sacrifice for the world (Acts 2:23). He is the "breath of God" giving inspiration to the Word of God (2 Timothy 3:16). When the names of the Father and Son are mentioned, the Holy Spirit is mentioned equally with them (Matthew. 28:19, 20). He was part of the incarnation of Christ (Matthew. 1:18, 20). He is the agent of regeneration at the time of salvation, enabling us to be born again (Titus 3:5). Because He is God, He can be blasphemed, which leads to eternal damnation (Mk. 3:29). These and many other references show without doubt that the Holy Spirit is God.

Matthew 28:18-20 gives us an interesting look at the deity of the Holy Spirit. In these verses, Jesus gave the Great Commission to the disciples and the church. He refers to the three persons of the Trinity being involved, but seems to set the Holy Spirit aside for special emphasis

Christ declared that He has all power, or that He is omnipotent. The power of Christ is emphasized through the work of the Holy Spirit. Christ has promised by His omnipresence to be with us always. The continual presence of Christ is known through the indwelling of the Holy Spirit. In His omniscience, Christ knows the end from the beginning. Because the Holy Spirit knows all things, He guides us to the fulfillment of the will of God.

Reflection: As you worship, spend time honoring the Holy Spirit as God, and recognize who He is to you, out loud.

Day 5

The Dove
Genesis 8:6-12

The Bible is filled with symbols. But it is important to remember that symbols are shadows of a greater truth, and enhance the study of God's word. They don't form doctrine.

In Scripture, the dove is a symbol of the gentle nature of the Holy Spirit. The most important reference to this is found at the baptism of Jesus. The Father spoke from heaven, and the Holy Spirit descended upon Jesus in the form of a dove (Matthew. 3:16-17). This speaks of Jesus's empowerment into ministry—an example for all of us.

The first reference to the dove appears in the story of the Genesis flood. Noah had endured the judgment of God, tucked away safely in the ark. After the flood receded, he tried to determine if it was safe to exit. To find this out, he sent forth two birds to bring proof that the earth was safe to dwell upon. He first sent a raven, which never returned to the ark.

Noah later sent a dove. The first time the dove was sent, it simply returned to the ark, having found no place to rest. The second time the dove was sent, it came back with an olive branch. The third time Noah sent the dove, it found a place to dwell, and did not return.

This is a beautiful picture of the Holy Spirit. In the Old Testament, He was sent to enable individuals for mighty deeds. However, He did not permanently indwell them. When Christ came, the Holy Spirit was sent to dwell in Christ, enabling Him to finish His work. By the Spirit's power, Christ ascended to the Father with the olive branch of peace and redemption. Finally, the Holy Spirit was sent to the church, empowering it and permanently indwelling, and assisting it to fulfill the Great Commission.

Reflection: The Holy Spirit is a gentleman. We should not be frightened by the work of the Holy Spirit in our lives. Yield to His work in your life today.

Day 6

The Oil
Psalm 133

Another symbol of the Holy Spirit is oil. Oil produced from olives or a mixture of spices was an important part of Old Testament worship culture. For instance, it was used to supply the golden candlestick of the Tabernacle and Temple with light (Exodus35:8). The Holy Spirit is the oil that we must constantly replenish in our lives to keep us burning brightly for the glory of God.

Special anointing oil reserved specifically for the priesthood was poured over them as they were ordained for Temple worship. It became an agent of service and separation as it differentiated the common from the sacred. A beautiful picture of this is found in Psalms 133, where we see a celebration of the anointing of the High Priest, Aaron. The oil was poured on Aaron's head, and then flowed down to his clothes. The result is good and pleasant unity according to verse one.

The High Priest with a greater ministry than that of Aaron of the Old Testament is Jesus Christ. He was anointed with the Spirit to accomplish His ministry, (Acts 10:38) and continues it to this day. Not only has Christ been anointed, but so has

His body—the church. Just as the oil flowed from Aaron's head to his body, so has the Holy Spirit been poured on our head—Jesus Christ. Then, the oil flowed down to His body—the church—on the Day of Pentecost (Acts 2).

Every believer has been called into a new priesthood of God (Isaiah 61:6; 1 Peter 2:9). We are to carry an anointing that differentiates us from the world. The same empowerment our High Priest Jesus experienced is available for us to accomplish greater things for God's glory (John 14:12).

Reflection: The Holy Spirit was given to the church as a whole by being given to each individual believer. Ask God to fill the local body of believers with His Spirit by filling individuals with the Spirit.

Day 7

The Wind
John 20:22

The study of the Holy Spirit is called, Pneumatology. This is from the Greek word Pneuma, meaning breath or wind which is one of the most common pictures of the Holy Spirit in Scripture.

When God created man out of the dust of the ground, he was a lifeless form unable to function until God breathed into him, and he began to live. This is the pattern that God uses in our lives. Before we come to know Christ as our personal Savior, we are spiritually dead without a purpose in our life. (Ephesians 2:1) But the process of salvation is what Jesus called being "born again." When Jesus was asked how a person could enter the kingdom of God, He said that one must be born again of the Spirit. He then used the blowing of wind to show that God moves to do his will including our salvation. God uses His Spirit to not only regenerate us, but to also perform His will. (John 3:1-8)

In the Scripture reading for this day, Jesus "breathed" on those gathered before His ascension, and commanded them to receive the Holy Spirit. It is ironic that Jesus "breathed" on them associating the Holy Spirit filling their lives with the breath of God. Interestingly enough, on the Day of Pentecost when the Holy Spirit was given to the church, the description given of the experience was like a rushing wind. The Holy Spirit swept into their lives like a mighty wind, and filled them.

We need the wind of the Spirit to move on our lives all the time. Paul wrote to Timothy and encouraged him to rekindle the gift of the Holy Spirit. The idea is that Timothy's walk with God was like a fire that had burned down to glowing coals. What reignites the coals? The wind of the Spirit does. May the wind of the Spirit reignite our hearts to once again burn brightly for the glory of God. (II Timothy 1:6)

Reflection: If a passion for God is not a priority in your life, begin to earnestly seek God for a personal revival through a fresh touch from the Holy Spirit.

Day 8

The Fire
Matthew 3:11; Luke 3:16

God is described as a consuming fire (Hebrews 12:29). Since the Holy Spirit is God, He at times has manifested Himself by use of fire.

There are several ways the Holy Spirit is seen in relation to fire. The Holy Spirit is the fire of God's judgment. In the devotional readings for today, descriptions of the infilling of the Holy Spirit is immediately followed by God separating the wheat from the useless chaff which is then burned. The empowerment of the Holy Spirit in a person's life means there is a constant separation of the clean from the unclean. Isaiah calls it the spirit of judgment and the spirit of burning. (Isaiah 4:4)

The Holy Spirit is also the fire of God giving direction to our lives. When Israel left Egypt heading for the land of promise, God led them with His presence as a cloud by day, and a pillar of fire by night. (Psalms 78:14) Only when the presence of God moved were they to move.

The Holy Spirit is the fire for our ministry. Isaiah was used by God for the first five chapters of the prophetic book he wrote. It was not until He experienced the life changing presence of God in His life at the altar of sacrifice did he truly find his voice. While recognizing His need for God's cleansing, a coal of fire was taken from the altar, and applied to his lips. He was made clean, and sent on a prophetic mission. (Isaiah 6:6-8)

In our ministry as believers, our lives need the fire of the Holy Spirit to not only cleanse us and direct us, but we need the Holy Spirit to burn within us to accomplish ministry. When the Holy Spirit came in Acts chapter two, it is described as tongues of fire resting upon each recipient individually. Not only were they filled with the Spirit, they also found their voice.

Reflection: We should be burning with a burden for ministry. Ask the Holy Spirit to fill you with His fire to finish the job you are commissioned to do.

Day 9

A Temple for the Holy Spirit
I Corinthians 6:19-20

We were created by God to enjoy the closeness of His fellowship. By our willful choice, sin has separated us from Him, and has blocked our access to the fulfillment of His presence. The process of salvation is God bridging the gap for a restored relationship with lost creation.

Examples of this is seen when God commanded Moses to build a tent in which He could dwell with Israel. (Exodus 25:8) When Moses finished the construction, God filled it with His glory. (Exodus 40:34-35) King David longed so much for God that he had the greatest symbol of God's presence—the Ark of the Covenant—brought to Jerusalem. There he built a special tent for it to dwell in so he could have access to God's presence. He later commissioned his son Solomon to build an elaborate Temple for God. When Solomon dedicated the temple, God filled it with His presence. But these tents and buildings limited mankind's access to God. God was restricted to one nation (Israel), one tribe within that nation (Levi), and one man within that tribe (high priest).

God has provided once and for all access to His presence. John 1:14 says that Jesus came to dwell among us. This means literally that He "pitched His tent" with us. He became human, and was filled with the Holy Spirit. By His death on the cross and resurrection, the wall separating us from God was torn down allowing access to God's presence. (Matthew. 27:51; Hebrews 4:14-16)

When the Holy Spirit came in Acts chapter two, it was absolute proof that God no longer dwells among us in man-made buildings. His temple is now our body. He fills us and lives within us through the indwelling of the Holy Spirit in restored fellowship and communion. Our duty as believers is to separate our bodies as instruments for the glory of God.

Reflection: In what ways are you bringing discipline into your life so that God may use you to bring Him glory?

Day 10

Rivers of Living Water
John 7: 37-39

The context of today's Scripture reading centers on the Feast of Booths. This Jewish holiday was a wonderful time for remembering the goodness of God in sending the harvest, remembering how God had brought the Jewish forefathers through forty years of wilderness wandering, and to remember the coming of Israel's restoration and glory. They knew this reign of peace and prosperity would be instituted by the return of the Messiah, and a river of living water flowing from Jerusalem. (Zac. 14:8)

When Jesus stood up on the last day of the feast and proclaimed that living waters would proceed from those who believed in Him, He was actually proclaiming Himself as Messiah, and that the Kingdom of God had arrived. Some rightfully suggested that Jesus was the Messiah. (v.41)

At the same time, Jesus was referring to the sending of the Holy Spirit in relation to the Kingdom being established. This was not new to Jewish thinking. God had promised a Spirit outpouring during the Kingdom reign through the prophets, and the outpouring would be like water to a thirsty desert. (Isaiah 32:15) Jesus was really saying that the Kingdom's blessings are available through the giving of the Holy Spirit to those willing to believe and receive.

Note the progression Jesus used in receiving the Holy Spirit. First, there must be a thirst for God. Secondly, come to Jesus. Thirdly, believe according to the Scriptures. Fourth, receive the gift. This progression leads to being filled with the Spirit, and experiencing the kingdom blessings and gifts. The King and Kingdom have come, and are made available to us through the Holy Spirit filling our lives.

Reflection: For what things do you hunger and thirst? Are they spiritually based or fleshly based? Write down the desires of your life, and fit them into categories of either "for me" or "for God."

Day 11

The Seven Spirits
Isaiah 11:1-2; Revelation 1:4

The kingdom of God is governed by the government of God. That is, the laws of the kingdom govern the heart of every believer. As a result, the character, attitude, and person of God will be manifested to the world through the lives of Christians. Salvation of a true believer begins with the release of self-rights, and the proclamation of Jesus Christ as Lord. What we get in return as stewards of God's resources is far greater than what we could have within ourselves.

Within the government of God, the Father, Son, and Holy Spirit have differing roles. The Father has various workings and operations that He establishes. The Son has administrative roles in which He controls. And the Holy Spirit disperses the grace or gifts of God. (I Cor. 12:3-6) At the same time, the Father, Son, and Holy Spirit are One and in total agreement. With the Father on the throne and the Son seated beside Him, the Holy Spirit is before the throne described in Revelation as the seven Spirits. (Rev. 1:4)

This doesn't mean there are seven Holy Spirits. That would be heresy. In Scripture, the number seven is given the meaning of divine perfection. No matter how the Holy Spirit manifests Himself, He will always do so with perfection in every way. These seven spirits are manifestations of the Holy Spirit in fulfilling the will of God. They are seen in the life of Jesus Christ and are as follows: The spirit of the Lord, the spirit of wisdom, the spirit of understanding, the spirit of counsel, the spirit of might, the spirit of knowledge, and the spirit of the fear of the Lord. They are to be manifested in our lives as we live out the Kingdom of God fulfilling the mandate for our lives.

Reflection: If any one lacks wisdom, we are told to ask God to give it to us abundantly. (James 1:5) If you lack any of the gifts of God, ask Him to give them to you in a liberal way.

Day 12

Authority of the Spirit
Zechariah 4:1-14

The Book of Zechariah is filled with amazing symbolism, and chapter four is a great example. A Jewish remnant had been sent back to Jerusalem after 70 years of captivity. Life for the population had begun with commerce and building of personal dwellings. But, opposition from within and without had hindered the building of the temple. Zechariah is encouraged by the Lord that the Temple will be built, and that it wouldn't be by the might of man or the power of man, but by the Spirit of the Lord.

The Scripture reading today contains a beautiful picture of the work of the Holy Spirit. There is an allusion to the golden lampstands that belonged in the temple receiving oil directly from two olive trees planted next to them. (vs. 2, 3, 12-13) Although probably referring to a specific prophet and priest, it also speaks to us as believers of our need for a constant infilling of the oil of the Spirit in our lives. Without a fresh touch of the Spirit in our lives, we tend to do the work of God in our own might and power with the result being burnout, stress, and fatigue.

Jesus knew what it meant to be constantly filled with the Holy Spirit. Immediately after His baptism in water and being filled with the Spirit, He was taken to the wilderness for a 40 day fast and temptation. When He came forth from this time of extreme spiritual battle, it is noted that He returned filled with the power of the Spirit. (Luke. 4:1, 14) He entered the wilderness filled with the spirit, and came out filled.

A wilderness experience is no time to be less dependent on the work of the Holy Spirit in our lives. Our relationship with the Holy Spirit will only grow stronger as we depend on Him. He takes the mountains in our life and brings them down by His grace. (Zechariah 4:7)

Reflection: Are you facing a mountain in your life? The Holy Spirit will make a way where there seems to be none as you trust in Him today.

Day 13

A Holy Spirit Outpouring
Isaiah 32:14-20

The church needs to awaken, and once again become a force for truth and righteousness. Our families need to be restored and become a force for stability. Our communities need to change, so justice can be realized among the disadvantaged. Unless there is change and people turn toward God and His Word, there will be no order, no peace, and no justice.

The change agent that can restore normalcy back to culture is revival. And revival comes when people turn to God in repentance and humility. God has promised to send His Spirit to restore what has been taken away. (II Chron. 7:14)

The Scripture reading from the Book of Isaiah for this devotion is a picture of a society that had lost its way. The results were devastating. Nothing man could do remedied the problem. Without a change toward righteousness, there was no hope.

Then the Holy Spirit was poured out from above. That which was like a wilderness was changed to be like a field yielding plenty of fruit. The fruit was made up of peace, righteousness, justice, and security. (vs. 17-18)

The Holy Spirit enables us to have fruit and a harvest in our lives. That which we have sown to the Spirit will bring a harvest no matter the circumstances that surround us. Man-made remedies to our problems may fail, but the Holy Spirit can change us eternally.

Isaiah concludes the chapter by reminding us that Spirit filled people sow into various missions (waters) by sending out laborers (oxen) to help bring in the harvest.

Reflection: What are you doing for the cause of missions? Are you sowing of your time and treasure to send the gospel? Ask God for a great harvest.

Day 14

What is the Spirit Saying to You?
Revelation 2:7

The book of Revelation is divided up into three distinct sections. There is reference to the things that have happened, the things that are happening now, and the things that will happen later. (Rev. 1:19) Within the section dealing with the things happening now, there are seven churches that are specifically addressed with special warnings and commendations. At the conclusion of addressing each church, there is an admonition to make sure to listen to what the Spirit is saying.

This is important not only because the Spirit of God is saying something, but because the Holy Spirit uses human vessels in which to speak. This is one of the results of being Spirit filled. Spirit filled individuals not only have an ear to hear what the Spirit is saying, they also receive a voice for proclaiming what the Spirit is saying. This is a New Testament pattern repeated multiple times. Note these examples:

> 1. Elizabeth (mother of John the Baptist) was filled with the Spirit, and prophesied. (Luke. 1:41)
> 2. Zacharias (father of John the Baptist)

was filled and prophesied. (Luke. 1:67)

3.   Simeon was in the Temple, and the Holy Spirit was dwelling upon him. When he saw the baby Jesus, He prophesied a blessing. (Luke. 2:25)

4.   After Jesus was filled with the Spirit at His first public appearance, He preached because He was anointed with the Spirit. (Luke. 4:18)

5.   Believers spoke in tongues, and preached when the Holy Spirit filled them. (Acts 2:4)

Reflection: Many Spirit filled individuals don't allow the Holy Spirit to speak through them. As you spend time alone with God, ask Him to open your heart to receive a word from the Lord. Then share it with another believer.

Day 15

What is the Spirit Saying to You?
Matthew 10:20

The verse of Scripture used for this devotion comes within the context of Jesus commissioning His disciples to spread the gospel of the Kingdom. He warned them that they could be brought before governmental authorities for their witness, and if that happened, they were to allow the Holy Spirit to speak for them. Then Jesus explained that the Holy Spirit speaking for them was in reality the Father speaking for them

Most of the time when individuals speak, they express their thoughts from a human point of reference. The unregenerate mind is centered on a fallen worldview, and most communication is corrupted. When a person accepts Christ into their life and is born of the Spirit, they think differently. Their mind becomes kingdom focused, and should express the mind of Christ. (Philippians. 2:5; 4:8) The Holy Spirit changes a person's way of thinking and communicating.

The means by which God allows us to approach His throne is through the agency of prayer. Because we live in a broken and fallen world and have a body susceptible to weakness and pain, there are times when we don't know how we should pray. We need the Holy Spirit to speak for us. According to the book of Romans, the Holy Spirit is our helper and He intercedes through us, praying the will of God. (Romans 8:26-27) The book of Jude alludes to this by encouraging prayer in the Spirit. (Jude 20)

There are also times that we don't have the wisdom and knowledge to know what we should do in relation to a decision. Thankfully, several of the gifts are words from the Spirit to give us wisdom and knowledge. They are called the words of wisdom and knowledge. (I Cor. 12:8)

Reflection: Do you have the mind of Christ? Do you think the thoughts of God? Engraft God's word in your heart, and then speak them and pray them.

Day 16

The Double Portion
II Kings 2:13, 14

Elijah was a mighty prophet of the Lord used in the Old Testament to bring an awakening to the nation of Israel. The ministry of Elijah was filled with many miracles resulting from a life of prayer. (James 5:17, 18)

Near the end of Elijah's ministry, he realized that his prophetic calling would need to be passed to another person. He chose a man by the name of Elisha to be his protégé. The beginning of this mentoring process started when Elijah came to Elisha, and placed upon him his mantle of authority. Elisha destroyed the instruments of his occupation, and began the process of becoming a prophet of the Lord.

As time drew near for the ministry of Elijah to be over, he asked what Elisha would want as a parting gift. Elisha replied with a request for a "double portion" of Elijah's spirit. (II Kings 2:9) Elijah promised the request would be granted if Elisha were to see the occurrence of the great prophet being taken away. Finally, while closely following Elijah, Elisha saw the breathtaking event of Elijah taken to heaven in a fiery chariot. As

Elisha watched, a mantle fell from heaven to the ground. Elisha took the mantle and with it began his own ministry that would see many wonderful miracles.

This is a beautiful picture of the believer receiving the empowerment of the Holy Spirit. We must first be touched by Jesus at salvation when the mantle of the Holy Spirit is wrapped around our lives. The result is a call to leave the old life behind, and follow Jesus toward a prophetic destiny. But it can only happen because Jesus has ascended to the Father, and the mantle of the Holy Spirit has been sent down to us. By receiving the mantle of the Holy Spirit, we can do the works of the ascended Christ and even greater. (John 14:12)

Reflection: The secret of Holy power is found in a close relationship with Christ. A close relationship with Christ is found in the secret place of prayer. Where is your secret place and have you spent time there today?

Day 17

The Forty Day Dilemma
Acts 1: 2-9

Over 500 individuals were witnesses of the unchangeable proof that Jesus had truly resurrected from the grave. He not only proved His existence, but also poured into the lives of His disciples many wonderful concepts and principles concerning the Kingdom of God. Even though He was the resurrected Lord, He still depended on the work of the Holy Spirit in His life all the way to His ascension. (v.2)

At the end of 40 days, Jesus instructed His disciples to go back to Jerusalem and wait for the sending of the Holy Spirit. And then He ascended to Heaven. Now, the followers of Jesus faced a problem. Should they continue on to Jerusalem to wait for the Holy Spirit, or was the 40 day journey up to the ascension enough?

The number 40 holds a special lesson in Scripture. Moses spent 40 years of his life in the wilderness before he became leader of Israel's deliverance from Egypt. The nation of Israel wondered 40 years in the wilderness before going into the Promised Land. Jesus experienced 40 days of wilderness temptation before entering His ministry.

The 40 day ascension of Jesus created the opportunity for the disciples to reach their destiny. They had to confront the temptation to continue as usual with their life, or go the extra mile to obtain the promise. So it is with us. The promise of the Holy Spirit is for those who are willing to pay the price to pursue the blessings of God. While 40 days with Jesus may seem adequate, the seeker for more of God knows it is not enough. In their search, they soon discover that God still rewards those that diligently seek and wait for the infilling of the Holy Spirit. (Hebrews 11:6)

Reflection: Not only did the seekers take the steps necessary to the promise of the Spirit, they also prayed continually, (Acts 1:14) and were in the Word of God. (Acts 1:15-20) Do you have a daily reading plan of Scripture? If not, start today.

Day 18

We Owe a Debt
II Kings 4:1-7; Romans 1:14, 15

In the Old Testament there is a story about a woman whose husband had passed away, and left her the inability to support her family. The situation was so bad that she was on the verge of losing everything—including her sons who would be sold as servants to pay for her debts. She consulted with the prophet Elisha for help. He asked for any item of value within the house, and was given a vessel with oil.

The prophet then had the lady find as many empty vessels as possible from the neighbors. She miraculously poured into all the borrowed vessels an unending stream of oil until they were full. The oil was then sold to pay the woman's debts. And there was plenty of oil left for the widow's household.

This story is a picture of the church in need of paying the debt that it owes to the world. Paul knew his debt was to the "Jews and Greeks," (Romans 1:14-15) and that it was his mission to make sure the message of the gospel was given to them.

As believers, our mission is to make sure the message of salvation is given to the world. But we cannot give it unless we have vessels filled with the oil of the Holy Spirit. Jesus indicated that the Holy Spirit's coming would propel us not only into the locale we live, but also to the remotest parts of the earth. (Acts 1:8) The debt that we owe to unbelievers is large, but the potential to pay is found within the local church. Empty vessels must be found. They must be filled with the Spirit, and sent into the world. It is then that the mission's debt will be paid.

Reflection: What is your heart towards world and local missions? Do you give? Are you burdened for souls without Christ? Can you go? Spirit filled individuals have a drive for Missions in their heart.

Day 19

Simeon and the Holy Spirit
Luke 2:25-27

Every aspect of the life of Jesus Christ was permeated with the Holy Spirit. At the time of His birth, the Holy Spirit was significantly involved. When Mary was found to be with child, her future husband—Joseph—was told by an angel that the child was conceived of the Holy Spirit. (Matthew. 1:20)

When Mary the mother of Jesus met with Elizabeth the mother of John the Baptist, she was filled with the Holy Spirit, (Luke 1:41) Elizabeth's husband Zacharias was also filled with the Holy Spirit. (v.67)

Eight days after His birth, Jesus was presented to the Lord at the Temple according to the requirements of Jewish law. He was met there by a man named Simeon. This godly man was a person of great character. He had been waiting for the Messiah to come. Several things are mentioned about the work of the Holy Spirit in the life of Simeon.

> 1. The Holy Spirit dwelt on him. This indicates that Simeon was living close to the Lord, and God had His hand on Simeon's life.

2. The Holy Spirit revealed to Him that He would see Jesus Christ. His life was filled with revelation from God illuminating the coming Messiah.
3. The Holy Spirit led Him to Jesus. Because he followed the voice of the Spirit, he was able to see and prophetically confirm the future of Jesus.

Simeon is a wonderful example of how our lives can be dominated by the work of the Holy Spirit. Instead of dwelling upon us, the Holy Spirit now dwells within us. He wants to give us greater revelation of Jesus Christ, and to guide us to what Jesus can be for our lives.

Reflection: Spend time worshipfully waiting in the presence of God. It is from this that we receive revelation through the Holy Spirit.

Day 20

Jesus and the Holy Spirit
Acts 10:38

As previously noted, the Holy Spirit was important in the ministry of Jesus Christ. When He was ushered into this world, it was done through the work of the Holy Spirit. When He began His ministry, it was directed through the agency of the Holy Spirit working in His life. From the instant that the Holy Spirit as a dove descended to His baptism, Jesus was under the control of the Holy Spirit to accomplish the will of the Father. (Hebrews 10:7)

The first action of the Holy Spirit was to take Jesus into a wilderness temptation. It is interesting to note that Jesus was full of the Holy Spirit when He was led into this experience. There, He confronted and overcame—by the Word of God and empowerment of the Spirit—the desires and pride of the flesh nature. After the temptation, He returned not defeated or discouraged, but empowered by the Holy Spirit. (Luke. 4:1, 14)

The first ministry assignment of Jesus was to teach and preach the message of the Kingdom of God. His message carried a tone that attracted the attention of those that heard it. He was Holy

Spirit anointed, and His voice became a prophetic utterance. It was good news to the poor, to the captive, and the blind. The time of God's favor had arrived, and it was through the ministry of the Holy Spirit. (Luke. 4:17-22)

Jesus depended on the Holy Spirit for fellowship with the Father. Through the Holy Spirit, He experienced joy and spontaneously offered praise to the Father. (Luke. 10:21) This is an insight into a cherished part of Christ's life, and a glance at the future work of the Holy Spirit. He fills individuals with gladness for God, and they praise His wondrous works in the languages of many nations. (Acts 2:11, 26)

Reflection: Is your heart filled with the joy of the Holy Spirit? Has your heart overflowed in praise for the greatness of God? Give praise and adoration to God, and let it overflow in worship.

Day 21

The Father's Gift
Luke 11:13

God is full of grace, and loves to give gifts to His children when they ask for them. This is true in relation to all the gifts—especially with the gift of the Holy Spirit. The gift of the Spirit is available, yet, so many don't ask to receive it. The Scripture shows us simple steps to follow in regard to receiving the blessings the Father has for His children.

1. Since the Father's gifts are really an extension of Himself and His grace, they must be asked for with a heart filled with faith. (Romans 10:9-10)

2. The Father loves to reward His children when they are alone with Him in a secret place. (Matthew 6:6)

3. When we abide in Christ, we can ask the Father for the Holy Spirit, and He will give the gift to us. (John 15:16; 16:23)

4. The giving of the Holy Spirit is also referred to as the Promise of the Father. Whenever God promises something, He always honors His word. (Luke 24:49; Acts 1:4)

5. Not only are we to ask for the gift of the Spirit, but we are to ask in the name of Jesus. (John 14:26; 15:26)

6. God will give to those who fervently desire the gift of the Spirit. (Matt. 5:6)

7. Jesus always has His prayers answered. He asked the Father to send the Holy Spirit, and in Acts chapter two He was sent. (John 14:16; Acts 2:33)

Reflection: It is important that believers develop a relationship with the heavenly Father. Let your prayer life develop to the point that your most cherished times are with the Father.

Day 22

The Last Words of Jesus
John 14:15-16

The Last Supper had ended. The disciples were gathered around Jesus a bit confused about the events that had taken place. In an act of service, Jesus had washed their feet, and indicated that one among them would betray Him. Jesus spoke of things closest to His heart before the passion and death that were soon to take place. The thing He talked about the most concerned the Holy Spirit.

Jesus first referred to the Holy Spirit as the Paracletos, or one that comes alongside to advise and help. This indicated that the ministry of Jesus was about to transition. Even though Jesus told the disciples that He would be leaving them, they did not quite grasp it. Only after Jesus had ascended to Heaven, did the disciples see the importance of the ever present Holy Spirit.

Through the Holy Spirit, the disciples discovered that intimacy and fellowship with Jesus was not lost with His ascension. The Holy Spirit was sent to fill that role. Jesus had dwelt with them, but the Holy Spirit would dwell within them in the same love and fellowship they had with Jesus. (Philippians 2:1)

Jesus also indicated to the disciples that it was important they obey the commandments given to them, not only through the moral law of God, but the commandments He had handed down to them during His ministry. The various times Jesus had spoken about issues dealing with the Law of God had not only confirmed them, but had enhanced them. (Matthew 5:17-20) By sending the Holy Spirit, not only would the disciples be reminded of the commands of the Lord, but the Holy Spirit would also write them upon their hearts. A heart of obedience to the Word of God is also the heart that the Holy Spirit will do His greatest work.

Reflection: Did you have fellowship with the Holy Spirit today? If not, spend time in the Word, and in prayer listening for the voice of the Spirit.

Day 23

The Spirit as our Teacher
John 14:25-26

Jesus had indicated in John 13 that He would be with the disciples a short time, and then He would be taken from them. Jesus wouldn't physically be with them, but there would be two things they would always have: the words He had spoken, and the Holy Spirit.

After the ascension of Jesus into Heaven, the believers had only the Old Testament, and the teachings of Christ to explain the gospel. They would need the Holy Spirit to bridge the gap to the new covenant that Jesus had stablished with them at the last supper. (I Cor. 11:25)

Interestingly enough, about one tenth of the New Testament is made up of Old Testament quotations. When Peter preached the first sermon after the sending of the Holy Spirit in Acts chapter two, he used verse after verse from the Old Testament to prove that Jesus had indeed fulfilled the requirements of God for mankind's salvation.

New truth was given to the Apostles by the inspiration of the Holy Spirit. This message of the gospel would complement the death, burial, and resurrection of Christ. (Romans 15:4; I Cor. 15:1-4)

The Apostle Paul not only extensively used the Old Testament in his writings, but also included mysteries that were revealed to Him by the Holy Spirit. There are over ten mysteries, and include the resurrection (I Cor. 15:51), rapture (I Thess. 4: 13-18), and the church (Ephesians 3:3,10).

The Holy Spirit represents us before God, and represents God to us. He does this in opening the Word of God, and teaching us what it says and what it means to us in everyday life.

Reflection: For every situation in life that you have a question, the Word of God has an answer. Ask the Holy Spirit for revelation of the Word to reveal the principle and truth that will set you free.

Day 24

The Spirit of Truth
John 16:7-14

God is described in various ways such as Light and Love. But an aspect of His nature that many don't want to face is that God is Truth. Jesus is the Truth (John 14:6), and several times the Holy Spirit is referred to as the Spirit of Truth. (John 14:17; 15:26; 16:13) Truth makes us face the fact that we have broken the commandments of God, and deserve his judgment. It is then that we are convinced of our need of Christ's sacrifice, and rely on the grace of God to bring us into a right relationship with Him.

The Holy Spirit works against Satan on our behalf. Not only is the world judged, but the Prince of the World is judged. (John 16:11) Satan has been cast out by the work of Christ on the cross (John 12:31), and he has nothing in God. (John 14:30) Satan has no right to the people of God, because they are possessed by the Holy Spirit.

The Holy Spirit is also at work in the world drawing it to repentance. Jesus indicated that one of the roles of the Holy Spirit is to reveal sin as rebellion against God and His law. He convicts us of sin by use of the written law of God, the law written on our conscience, and laws governing nature. After convicting of sin, the Holy Spirit convinces the world of the need to be right before God. Of course, the only way to be right with God is through the righteousness of Jesus Christ. If the choice is not to accept the provision of salvation through Jesus Christ, the Holy Spirit will then bring condemnation or judgment. In other words, judgment will be based on whether a person accepted the truth, and whether they believed in the provision of salvation through Jesus Christ.

The Holy Spirit is the prophetic voice to the church. He speaks for Christ, glorifies Christ, and reveals the things of Christ. (John 16:13-14).

Reflection: We stand by the power of the Holy Spirit against the works of Satan. Claim the victory you have through the finished work of Christ.

Day 25

The Great Commission
Acts 1:8

Before Jesus was taken into Heaven, He accomplished several tasks. One was to prove that He was truly resurrected from the grave. This He did with convincing evidence. Another task was to give special instructions to the apostles. These orders were to encourage them to depend on the Holy Spirit to empower and guide them in accomplishing the responsibilities they were to confront in the future. (Acts 1:2, 4, 5).

When teaching about the Kingdom of God, Jesus related it to the sending of the Holy Spirit. Some questioned whether the Kingdom would be restored at that time. Jesus did not deny that the Kingdom would be restored, yet He deflected the question by indicating that the Father in heaven was in control of the world's future.

The concept that Jesus had in mind was for Spirit filled individuals to take the Gospel to the Kingdoms of the World. Note the following references:

> 1. Matthew. 28: 19 – The disciples were told to make disciples of all the nations, and to teach them to observe the commands of the Lord.

2. Mark 16:15 – The apostles were commanded to take the gospel to all nations.

3. Luke 24:47 – The message of forgiveness was to be preached to all nations.

4. Acts 1:8 – Believers were to take their witness to the far away parts of the earth.

Reflection: Jesus did not give us a "great suggestion." He gave us a "great commission." We are commanded to take the message of the gospel to the world. What are you doing to see this is done?

Day 26

Be Baptized with the Holy Spirit
Acts 1:5

Jesus commanded His followers to be baptized with the Holy Spirit. To accomplish the mission that Jesus laid out would require more than human effort and reasoning. It would require the power of God at work in the life of a believer.

It is interesting that Jesus compared the baptism of John with the baptism that would soon take place with the followers of Jesus. It was an immersion in water that propelled Jesus into His ministry, and it would be an immersion in the Holy Spirit that would propel the church into its ministry.

One aspect of the Holy Spirit baptism that is emphasized by Jesus is that it would be accompanied with power. In a direct reference to this, Jesus said that the Holy Spirit would cloth believers with power. (Luke 24:49) This power that would cloth believers is pictured in the life of Elisha. As the prophet Elijah was taken into Heaven, his mantle fell back to Elisha who picked it up, went forth, and accomplished great things for God. (See day 16)

Why is there an emphasis on power in relation to the Holy Spirit baptism? Jesus said in Acts 1:8

that when the Holy Spirit was come, those filled would receive power to be witnesses. Interestingly, the word witness is from the same Greek word that we get the word martyr. The Holy Spirit empowers us to not only have a voice for God, but to also give our lives for the message of the gospel.

It takes the empowerment of the Spirit to live every day as a witness for Jesus Christ. Through the Spirit, we see the miraculous take place as God spreads the message of His Kingdom.

Reflection: God is looking for someone who will step up and say, "Here I am Lord, use me." Will you be that one? Step out of your comfort zone and immerse yourself into ministry. Allow the Spirit to use you for the glory of God.

Day 27

They Were Filled with the Holy Spirit
Acts 2:1-4

Before the Holy Spirit came upon the disciples of Jesus Christ, they were gathered together as a corporate group. Being together as a unit kept their focus upon the waiting for the coming promise. While waiting, they also involved themselves in fervent prayer. (Acts 1:14) While with Jesus, they had learned that prayer to the Father was important to seeing results. They knew the mission would only be reached through the agency of prayer.

The Holy Spirit finally arrived. The believers were gathered in a house, and suddenly the presence of the Holy Spirit manifestly filled the room, and they were filled. With the coming of the Holy Spirit there were physical evidences. A sound came into the room like a mighty wind. Fire was distributed among those gathered, and they spoke with other tongues as the Holy Spirit gave them the utterance.

A visible manifestation of the Holy Spirit was not totally foreign to the mindset of those being filled. When the Tabernacle of Moses was built and dedicated, the presence of the Lord filled it.

When the Temple was built and dedicated, the presence of God filled it so thick that the priests were not able to minister. Now, the Holy Spirit fills individuals. They are the new tabernacle, or temple of God.

This Acts chapter two experience set in order a principle for those that receive the Baptism of the Holy Spirit. Peter described it in his sermon that followed as something seen and heard. (Acts 2:33) Later Peter and John were confronted by authorities regarding their powerful ministry, and both said they could only declare the things they had seen and heard. (Acts 4:20)

Reflection: Earnestly desire and expect God to fill you with the Holy Spirit by dedicating yourself to the Lord as a dwelling place of His presence. Wait on God and situate yourself for the empowerment God has for your life.

Day 28

They Spoke with other Tongues
Acts 2:1-4

No one knows for sure how many were filled with the Holy Spirit in Acts chapter two. The Scripture indicates that they were not only filled with the Holy Spirit, but the accompanying sign was they spoke with other tongues. The tongues in which they spoke were in the languages of various nations that had gathered for the Jewish feast of Pentecost.

It caused a stir in the city when those there heard their language being spoken. Some were amazed, and some were critical of what took place. Whether it was understood or not, the new church was now relevant to what was happening. If the church is to be able to affect the culture in which it is placed, it will need to speak the language of that culture. This is what the empowerment of the Holy Spirit does to a person. It enables them to be able to communicate the message of the gospel to whatever culture they belong.

At a previous time, God had decided that the nations of the world should be separated by mixing their languages. (Genesis 11:1-9) The result was people groups were scattered. God then called

Abraham to be the person in whom He raised up the nation of Israel, in which He could place His law and bring the Messiah. On Pentecost, God brought individuals from various places to form one body of believers—the church—made up of both Jews and Gentiles speaking the praises of God.

The fact that they spoke in tongues was important. Tongues now became the accompanying evidence of receiving the Holy Spirit. In a deeper sense, it became the avenue of speaking of the wonderful and mighty things of God. (Acts 2:11)

Reflection: When asking for the gift of the Spirit, allow God to fill you, and give you a voice or other tongue to speak of the wonderful things of God.

Day 29

What does this Mean?
Acts 2:12

Following the outpouring of the Holy Spirit, there was a mixed reaction by the bystanders. Some were amazed while others thought those filled with the Holy Spirit were drunk with new wine. Being accused of being filled with new wine is an interesting reaction to what took place. Jesus used earthen vessels to turn water into wine as the first miracle of His ministry. (John 2:1-11) Now, as the first miracle to the church, Jesus filled human vessels with what onlookers compared to new wine.

Peter stepped forward and spoke for the apostles. Fifty days earlier, He denied that he knew the Lord. Now with boldness—being filled with the power of the Spirit—he stood before a large group of individuals and prophetically spoke. He informed the crowd that those filled with the Spirit were simply experiencing what had long ago been prophesied by the Prophet Joel. He connected it to the last days and prophecy—the beginning of a new dispensation. He spoke of how God would use young men with a vision for the future. He also spoke of older men who would give God's dream as it related to the past. He connected the

Pentecost experience to every people group no matter the gender or age. (Acts 2:16-18)

The sermon that Peter preached was centered on the gospel message. He spoke of the death of Jesus (Acts 2:23), the burial of Jesus (Acts 2:27), the resurrection of Jesus (Acts 2:31), and the ascension of Jesus (Acts 2:34). He summed up the sermon with a statement that Jesus was indeed the Lord and Messiah. (Acts 2:36)

The result was about three thousand individuals were convicted of their sins by the Holy Spirit, and repented. The church was formed, filled with the Holy Spirit, and immediately became a witness to the world.

Reflection: If you are called by God to salvation, believe Him for the infilling of the Holy Spirit. Then allow the Holy Spirit to use you as an instrument to tell others about what God has done for you. Where will you start?

Day 30

The Judgment of the Holy Spirit
Acts 5:1-11

The Holy Spirit not only filled individuals on the day of Pentecost, but He also formed them into a body of believers that assembled together for consistent teaching, fellowship, and worship. (Acts 2:42) This gathering of believers resulted in other outpourings of the Holy Spirit, and a great amount of God's grace being given. (Acts 4:31-33) In the midst of God's mighty move among His people, Satan was also at work.

Because believers felt that Jesus would return again at any time, it was not unusual for individuals to give their possessions to the apostles to be used for distribution among the poor. One couple sold their property and gave part of the proceeds to the Apostle Peter claiming that it was the sum total of what they had profited. The Holy Spirit revealed to Peter that the couple had lied about their giving. Peter severely confronted the couple, pronounced the judgment of God upon them, and they both died.

This may seem harsh, but the Holy Spirit was intent on making sure that the mission of the church was not destroyed by sin. The apostle Paul was very concerned about this, and warned leaders of churches to make sure they guarded not only God's flock, but their personal lives. Jesus Christ gave His blood to purchase the church, and it is the Holy Spirit that places leaders to oversee it. (Acts 20:28) If a sinful tendency is allowed to grow within the local church, it can destroy the witness and mission of that congregation. (I Cor. 5:8-9)

The Holy Spirit is also known as the Spirit of Holiness. (Romans 1:4) With the Holy Spirit infilling, a greater love for God develops, and reveals the contrasting effects of sin. It is then that we confront our personal sin for greater empowerment and grace of the Spirit.

Reflection: Do you have a godly hatred for evil. If not, ask God to allow you to see sin through His eyes. It will bring repentance.

Day 31

Signs and Wonders
Hebrews 2:4

The work of the Holy Spirit is unlimited because He is all powerful. When the gospel of the Kingdom is preached, there should be signs, wonders, miracles, and gifts of the Holy Spirit. These are vital in the life of the believer, and the function of the local church. They are especially vital in the missional spread of the gospel.

The ministry of Jesus had many signs, wonders, and miracles. With the sending of the Holy Spirit, the signs and wonders continued. Several times in the book of Acts, signs and wonders were part of the apostolic ministry. (Acts 2:43; 5:12; 14:3) In the ministry of the apostle Paul, there were signs and wonders through the power of the Holy Spirit. (Romans 15:19)

Why does there need to be signs and wonders in the church today? One reason is because God uses a "sign" to show a greater truth. The generation to which Jesus ministered was looking for a sign. Jesus gave them the sign of the life of Jonah as a pointer toward His own death and resurrection. Another reason is because God uses "wonders" to cause individuals to stop and think through the truth. When those that lied to the Holy Spirit were struck dead, everyone paused to contemplate the awesomeness of God, and the need to reverence Him. (Acts 5:11)

Signs and wonders happen best when the Holy Spirit invades the mundane and consistent nature of life with the miraculous. This is often done through the gifts of the Holy Spirit that have been given to the church. Whether it is healing, provision, or any other miracle, the Holy Spirit as God is able to suspend any law of nature, and make the impossible become possible.

Reflection: In obedience to God's word, take steps of faith and God will do the miraculous. What faith steps will you take today?

Day 32

The Initial Sign Evidence
Acts 10:45-46

As the church began to grow, its persecution grew as well. Persecution not only came from the religious establishment in Jerusalem, but also from the governmental authorities. Persecution was intended to stamp out the church, but it actually caused the church to spread.

As the church spread, so did the witness of the gospel. It was to the Jews first in Jerusalem, and then to Judea and Samaria like Jesus commanded. (Acts 1:8) But the witness of the gospel, and the work of the Holy Spirit were intended not only for Jews, but Gentiles as well. The deacon Philip was miraculously sent to an Ethiopian to preach the gospel, and a conversion took place. Later, Peter was sent to an Italian to preach the gospel, and he was also converted. The missional command of Jesus was being fulfilled by touching three people groups representing the continents of Asia, Africa, and Europe. The Holy Spirit was at work proving that a sign of being filled with the Holy Spirit was the spreading of the gospel.

But another sign preceded the voice of witness. When the believers were filled on the day of Pentecost, they spoke with other tongues. When Peter preached the gospel to the Roman commander, Cornelius not only received salvation, but was also filled with the Spirit, and spake with other tongues. (Acts 10:46) Later when the Apostle Paul ministered to the disciples at Ephesus, they were filled with the Holy Spirit, and spoke with other tongues and prophesied. (Acts 19:6) The pattern that developed from the book of Acts is that speaking with other tongues was the initial evidence of receiving the baptism of the Holy Spirit. While speaking in tongues is not the only evidence of receiving the Spirit, it is the initial evidence, and leads the believer to having a powerful prophetic voice for witnessing.

Reflection: Some make the mistake of seeking for tongues instead of the infilling of the Spirit. Seek Jesus and be filled with the Spirit. The rest will follow.

Day 33

The Holy Spirit and the Church
Acts 13:1-5

There is probably no local church in the Book of Acts that more represented the idea of ekklesia than the church at Antioch. They were not only called out of the world, but were called from various ethnic backgrounds. Barnabas was Jewish. Simeon was probably of African descent. Luke was a Greek doctor. Manaen was from a royal background. And Saul (later Paul) was a highly educated Asian.

They were also a church with a variety of ministry gifts. There were some within the church that had the gift of prophecy, and the gift of teaching. These ministry gifts were not only functional, but balanced.

It is at Antioch that we see the operation of the gifts of the Holy Spirit in the local church. The Antioch church had a deep commitment to prayer, personal discipline, and unity. From within this spiritual environment, the Holy Spirit spoke, and expressed that Barnabas and Saul were to be separated for a special work in which they were called. In agreement with the Holy Spirit and with one another, the church laid their hands on Barnabas and Saul, and then sent them into their ministry calling. But it was not just the church that sent them, it was the Holy Spirit. (Acts 13:4)

The role of the local church is to not only facilitate the discipleship and fellowship of believers, but it is to be a place where ministry takes place. Ministry is more than to believers, it includes ministry to God through prayer, spiritual discipline, and worship. The Holy Spirit will "show up" when believers gather in unity and in his name. (Matthew. 18:20) When God is in the midst of His people, He will minister and speak to those that are gathered. He will speak through the teaching and preaching of His word, and will prophetically confirm the call of those chosen for a specific work.

Reflection: God uses the local church to confirm the call of those chosen for ministry. In what ways are you staying active in a local church until the call is confirmed?

Day 34

The Holy Spirit in Ministry
Acts 11:24

The Book of Acts began with the outpouring of the Holy Spirit, but doesn't have a conclusion. The Holy Spirit has not quit working. The acts of the Holy Spirit continue to this day. The power of the Holy Spirit is needed to spread the message of the Kingdom of God around the world.

An interesting theme emerges from the Book of Acts, paralleling the empowerment of the Spirit. Not only are the gifts of the spirit manifested, but maturity became a theme as well. Note how the following verses show character traits accompanying the work of the Spirit:

1. Leaders were filled with the Spirit and also with wisdom. (Acts 6:3)
2. Believers walked in reverence and comfort of the Spirit. (Acts 9:31)
3. Individuals were filled with the Spirit and with faith. (Acts 11:24)
4. The disciples had the Spirit accompanied with joy. (Acts 13:52)

It is important that once believers are filled with the Holy Spirit, they continue to mature in their walk with the Lord. Some believe that the power of the Holy Spirit is all they need in their life to accomplish ministry. But if the character of God is not produced in daily life, there will be no power for ministry.

A great example of godly character is seen in the life of Barnabas. He helped establish the Antioch church, and mentored the future apostle Paul. He was known as a man of character, and led the first mission journey from Antioch. (Acts 13:2) Eventually Paul took the reins of leadership, but a person of character and Spirit led the way.

Reflection: Spiritual maturity and Spirit empowerment flow together. What spiritual disciplines do you feel the Holy Spirit is leading you to develop in your life? List them and seek God's help in improving in these areas.

Day 35

The Law of the Spirit of Life
Romans 8:1-4

Most bible students wouldn't think to make a study of the Holy Spirit from the book of Romans. But very few books of the Bible would match the information from Romans on the subject of the Holy Spirit especially the eighth chapter. This chapter alone contains at least fifteen references to the Holy Spirit involving various topics.

Right from the beginning of Romans 8, the Holy Spirit is shown as a direct part of our salvation. In the previous chapters of Romans, the life of a person dominated by the flesh nature, and living a life of condemnation is portrayed. It is a conclusion to the reality that everyone has sinned, and is under the penalty of death. (Romans 3:23; 6:23) This is called the law of sin and death, and simply states that sin leads to eternal death. (Romans 8:2)

Then hope springs forth as another law is introduced, and states that we can have freedom from the condemnation of sin. This law is called the law of the Spirit of life. It simply states that if a person is placed "in Christ," they are free from the law that states eternal death results from sin.

The principle of being "in Christ" is the most important theological consideration of the Apostle Paul writings. Being in Christ is accomplished through the work of the Holy Spirit when we are regenerated or "born again." (Titus 3:5) Before salvation, the heart is dead and unable to respond to God. (Ephesians 2:1) After salvation, the heart is made alive with the same Spirit that rose up Christ from the dead. (Romans 8:10-11) While the mind of an unbeliever is dominated by instinct and self-fulfillment, a regenerated person focuses on the things of the Holy Spirit. (Romans 8:6) While unable to keep God's law before salvation, a person that is regenerated keeps the law of God in Christ while walking in the Spirit. (Romans 8:4).

Reflection: Read Romans chapter 8 and circle each mention of the Holy Spirit. Then meditate on what these verses mean to you, and your walk with the Lord.

Day 36

The Spirit of Adoption
Romans 8:14-16

Before we were in the family of God, we were slaves bound by the spirit of bondage to the world, flesh, and the devil. Through the Spirit Of Adoption, we were placed into the family of God, and began a relationship with our heavenly Father as His child. Not only did we begin a relationship with the Father, but we are encouraged to pursue that relationship. As Romans 8:15 puts it, we are to appeal to Him as our Father. This appeal is to be emotional in nature, and would be as a small child crawling onto the lap of their earthly father, verbally expressing their love. Not a formal expression of love, but one that is comfortable, intimate, and reserved just for daddy.

Since the past life of a believer is filled with self-centered and sin-filled living, it is a constant battle to stay convinced that we are really loved by God as our Father. The beginning of Romans chapter eight states that there is no condemnation to a person in Christ and of the Spirit. Not only is a believer to trust in that, but they are to also allow the Holy Spirit to convince them that they are children of God. This is done as the Holy Spirit opens the Word of God to us, and transforms the way we think. We go from self-centered thinking to God-centered thinking. (Romans 12:1-2)

Involved with our relationship to the Father, we are made partakers of the inheritance reserved for His Son, Jesus Christ. The inheritance of Christ is seen in His suffering, resurrection, and glorification. For us to be partakers of the inheritance with Him, we must also be willing to endure the trials and tribulations of this life. Any suffering we may endure is nothing compared to the glory that we will inherit when we are glorified together with Him. (Romans 8:18)

Reflection: In your suffering, remember that you are being held in the arms of the Heavenly Father. Anything that comes against you will push you closer to Him. In your prayer time, give thanks to the Father for His unfailing love.

Day 37

Praying in the Spirit
Romans 8:19-23

Because sin entered into the world, creation is now under a curse. The earth on which we dwell endures the pain and travail of this curse. Since we are made from the earth, we endure as well. All creation—even humans—constantly deals with the results of the original sin through our endurance of life's hardships

Only a human redeemer could release the grip of sin and death on the earth and mankind. This was done when Jesus Christ came, and with His life, paid the price to release all creation from the curse. Although the price was paid, creation awaits His return so the transaction can be completed.

To an extent, the redemption process has been completed in the life of believers. The spirit of a believer is redeemed fully at salvation. The soul is daily being redeemed by the Word, and work of the Holy Spirit. The body will have full redemption at the return of Jesus Christ. (Romans 8:23)

In the meantime, we that have the Holy Spirit must live in a body awaiting the redemption process to be complete. The war between the flesh and spirit is a daily event. The spiritual struggle that results from fighting the works of darkness is an enduring conflict. But, we have hope in God. He is our faith in the future, and we access that hope by placing our trust in the work of the Holy Spirit and the Word of God.

To stay victorious in this life, a believer must have a consistent and powerful prayer life. One of the most wonderful ways to pray is to pray the will of God by praying in the Spirit. When a person prays in this manner, they allow themselves to be used as an instrument of intercession by the Holy Spirit.

Reflection: Do you have a consistent time set aside to seek the face of the Lord in prayer? If not, learn to develop prayer as a discipline of your life.

Day 38

The Holy Spirit as Our Helper
Romans 8:19-23

Prayer is not always an easy task. Frequently, we don't know how to pray, in regard to our prayer burdens. There are instances when we want to pray, but our heart is so heavy we are unable. It is at these times and others that we need an intercessor to represent us before the Father. While Jesus is our intercessor before the Father in Heaven, we are also represented before the Father by the Spirit.

The Holy Spirit is the One that Jesus referred to as our Helper. He comes along beside us to "help" us in the times of our weaknesses. The idea behind the Holy Spirit being our helper is that as we lift one end of a burden, the Holy Spirit lifts on the other end. We work together with the Holy Spirit as a co-laborer to accomplish the will of God.

While carrying our burdens in prayer, there are times we don't know how we should pray. The role of the Holy Spirit is to intercede for us with utterances that are too deep for our understanding. With the Spirit praying through us, He searches the heart and knows exactly how to intercede according to the will of God. While human intellect doesn't understand what is being said, the

Spirit speaks on our behalf, and for the will of God being fulfilled.

Praying in the Spirit is a powerful tool for a Spirit filled believer. Not only does it help in fulfilling the will of God, it also brings encouragement to the person praying. As the Book of Jude indicates, our faith is built up when we pray in the Holy Spirit. (Jude v.20)

We ultimately know that in the end, all things will work out for God's glory, and for those that love God and are called to His purpose. (Romans 8:28)

Reflection: When you come to the end of your ability to understand and articulate, allow the Holy Spirit to pray through you with groaning and utterances beyond your understanding.

Day 39

The Holy Spirit and Church Order
I Corinthians 12:4-12

The Apostle Paul used the human body as a means of illustrating the way the Church is to function. As a human body has many parts and those parts have different functions, so does the church.

This concept was important to members of the Corinthian church. They had split and splintered in their leadership, and were disorganized in the worship of God. (I Cor. 1:11-13) They were not disciplined, nor accountable in their function as a church, and there were many abuses. Paul addressed many of these abuses which included sexual misconduct, marriage dysfunctions, suing one another, and the misuse of the gifts of the Holy Spirit.

When Paul confronted the saints at Corinth about the use of the gifts of the Holy Spirit, his desire was not to remove them away from the church. Instead, he encouraged their use within the context of orderliness and accountability. He did this by explaining that each member of the trinity had a role within the church with the distribution of gifts. He showed that the Heavenly Father operated within and through the church with His gifts. (I Cor. 12:6; Romans 12:6-8) The Son, Jesus Christ, had ministry gifts that He administered through the local church. (I Cor. 12:5; Ephesians 4:11-12) And the Holy Spirit also had gifts that were important and distributed to believers within the local congregation within His sovereign will. (I Cor. 12:4; 8-11)

Paul combined the gifts of God together to show that they are all important. (I Cor. 12:28-30) He also showed that whoever had been blessed with a gift was not to use that gift to the exclusion of others, but that every gift and every member of the body was important. The common gift that was to be shared was love for one another. (I Cor. 13)

Reflection: What gifts does God have for your life? Do you use the gift God has given you for the furtherance of the Gospel and glory of God?

Day 40

Gifts of the Holy Spirit
I Corinthians 12:4-12

The Greek word translated for "gift" carries the idea that the gifts of the Spirit are a manifestation of God's favor. This is no surprise since salvation and every other gift we have from God is a work of His grace.

Since the Holy Spirit came in the book of Acts, there has been deliberation regarding the gifts. How they are to be used, when to be used, and the relevancy of the gifts are still a matter of debate. But the last word Paul left regarding the gifts of the Holy Spirit was that they are to be desired, especially if they are the greater gifts. (I Cor. 12:31)

There are nine gifts of the Holy Spirit listed in I Corinthians 12:4-12. The gifts can then be divided into the following three categories:

1. The Wisdom Gifts - Word of wisdom, word of knowledge and discerning of spirits.
2. The power gifts - faith, healings, and miracles.
3. The vocal gifts - Different kinds of tongues, interpretation of tongues, and prophecy.

Paul takes I Corinthians 14 to address the use of tongues, interpretation of tongues and prophecy. The conclusion he arrives is found at the end of the chapter where he promotes the pursuit of prophecy, and doesn't forbid the use of the gift of tongues. (I Cor. 14:39)

When Paul ended his dissertation on the gifts of the Holy Spirit, it is very plain that not only did he practice the use of the gifts within his personal life, but that the gifts are available from God for every believer, and should be orderly pursued. (I Cor. 12:31; 14:40)

Reflection: The Spirit has gifts for orderly function within the local church. As a Spirit filled person, how has God used your gifts to minister to others? Are you submitted to the local church leaders in use of the gift?

Day 41

Sealed by the Holy Spirit
II Corinthians 1:22; Ephesians 1:13, 4:30

At the time of salvation, believers are taken out of the Kingdom of Darkness, and placed into the Kingdom of Light. Whereas we were once slaves to sin and Satan, we have been purchased by the blood of Jesus Christ and now belong to Him. The assurance of our salvation and the security of it rests upon the foundation of the attributes of God. God knows everything and is all powerful. He knows those that belong to Him. Not only does He know those that are His, but He places His seal or identification mark upon them which is the Holy Spirit. (II Timothy 2:19) The enemy of our soul wishes to break that seal through temptation, condemnation, and guilt. But the Holy Spirit is committed to leading, keeping, and guiding us until the day He presents us faultless before God. (Jude 24)

The Holy Spirit also becomes the deposit within our lives as a down payment for the future. There are no words that can express the wonderful things God has prepared for those that love Him. (I Cor. 2:9) As a trust account in our lives, the Holy Spirit gives us a taste of what eternity will someday be. For instance, we have the promise in eternity of a new, incorruptible body. The deposit of the Holy Spirit within our lives is the promise of divine healing. In the future kingdom of God, we will know prosperity, peace, and blessing. In our lives now, the kingdom of God is within our hearts, and we experience many wonderful benefits of God. Through the deposit of the Holy Spirit, we are now able to have a sample of some of the future benefits of the Kingdom.

The Holy Spirit is the One who guarantees our blessings now, and in the future. When the final act of redemption is complete and the possession that is purchased by the blood is set free, we will fully know these blessings.

Reflection: The blessings that God has entrusted to us are accessed by faith. Ask in faith, and receive from the Lord the blessing that matches your need.

Day 42

The Holy Spirit and Victorious Living
Galatians 5:22-24

After salvation, the greatest need in a person's life is to change from being flesh and world oriented to thinking and acting like Jesus Christ. There are multitudes of people self-described as Christians, but their lifestyle proves they are not Christ followers. The true Christian experience is not centered on how we brand it. It is based on whether the Holy Spirit is enabling us to live out God's work of grace within our heart.

Paul began most of his letters by explaining the doctrinal side of God's work of salvation for man. His explanations are filled with theological insights that have amazed students of Pauline literature for centuries. At the same time, the end of Paul's writings is filled with practical ways of living out a godly lifestyle. The point being that theology is dead unless it can be put to practical use in everyday life. The Holy Spirit enables us to do that.

Every believer struggles with sinful desires. These desires or lusts will be with us until we pass from this life, or we are taken in the "catching away." (I Cor. 15:50-56) The indwelling of the Holy Spirit pulls the believer away from the actions of the flesh toward God's will. This clash between the flesh and the Spirit takes place within the soul. It affects the way we feel, the way we think, and the way we choose. (Galatians 5:16-18)

When a believer yields their will to follow the way of the Spirit, they will want to make right choices. Yielding to the Holy Spirit means the way one thinks is biblically based, and feelings become subservient to faith. Through time and patience, the fruit of the Spirit matures, producing Christ like character. It is a consistent and progressive work of the Holy Spirit and the Word of God. It is also known as sanctification. (Ephesians 5:26; II Timothy 2:21)

Reflection: As believers, we were placed in Christ and "in Christ" there is no sin. Set your heart on being like Christ by yielding to the power of the Spirit and the Word of God. How will this path to victory begin for you today?

Fruit of the Spirit
Galatians 5:22-24

Although there are places where one or two fruit are listed, there is only one full listing of the fruit of the Spirit in the Bible. In the book of Romans, joy and peace are used together in relation to the Holy Spirit. (Romans 14:17; 15:13) In the book of Ephesians the fruit of the Spirit is referred to in relation to light as contrasted to the unfruitfulness of darkness. (Eph. 5:9-11, II Cor. 6:6)

There are nine fruit of the Spirit, just as there are nine gifts of the Holy Spirit. When looking at the fruit of the Spirit, it must be noticed that they are described as fruit of the Spirit not fruits of the Spirit. One line of thinking is that since the fruit first mentioned is love it could mean that love is really the fruit of the Spirit, and the other characteristics are the fruit of love. Whether this is true or not, it must be noted that love is mentioned first and this means it is the most important; just as love is the most important part of the gifts of the Holy Spirit. (I Cor. 13:1-2) Without love our fruit and our gifts are nothing.

From the time of salvation, the fruit of the Spirit is proof of the development of godly character in a believer's life. (Romans 8:9) The fruit of the Spirit is a natural outgrowth of being attached to the True Vine which is Jesus Christ, and producing His character. (John 15:1-8)

The fruit of the Spirit is divided into the following categories:

1. Relationship with God—love, joy, and peace.
2. Relationship toward others—longsuffering, kindness, and goodness.
3. Relationship to ourselves—faithfulness, meekness, and self-control.

Reflection: Have you loved God with your whole heart and your neighbor as yourself? List practical ways of expressing the love of God to others.

Day 44

The Body and the Holy Spirit
I Corinthians 3:16; 6:19

The body is important to God. He is a spirit, and no person on Earth has seen Him and lived. (John 4:24) Jesus had a body prepared for His dwelling while on Earth, and because of the resurrection now has a glorified body. The Holy Spirit also has a body to dwell. It is called a Temple, and is the body of every born again believer.

A person that is born again has desires and tendencies that lean toward doing evil. These inclinations must be submitted to the power of Holy Spirit, disciplined, and brought under the Lordship of Jesus Christ. It is a lifelong process, and involves much hard work. The work we put into living out the work of the Spirit in our lives becomes a tool of witness to those without knowledge of Christ. As they see our good works, they will also see God and bring Him glory.

A temple is a place of worship, and this is what we are to do with our body. We must use it as an instrument of worship to God. Worship of God through the temple of our body is an enigma. We are told to offer it as a living sacrifice. Sacrifice normally means something that is dead, but in relation to our body it is to be alive, and participating in the worship process.

Not only is our body the temple of the Holy Spirit, but it is also a vessel. We are responsible for the care and purity of it as the dwelling place of the Holy Spirit. This is so important that Paul lets us know each individual believer will someday stand before Jesus Christ, and give an account of the works they have done for God. If they have built their life on the strong foundation on Jesus Christ, and used their temple to glorify God, there will be a great reward. For those that squander their life instead of investing in the work of God, although saved, they will not be rewarded. (I Cor. 3:9-15)

Reflection: Being physically healthy enables us to be more active in ministry. This requires personal discipline in diet, exercise, and not engaging in harmful practices. How are you in taking care of the Temple of the Spirit? How will you change?

Day 45

Things Not To Do
I Thessalonians 5:19

The Holy Spirit should always be worshiped and adored as God. But because He is looked at so often through the lens of experiential theology, many become too familiar with the things of God, and forget the importance of reverence and humility. Carelessly, the "God told me" excuse is used to defend human actions. Some even express prophetically what is claimed to be God's voice and equate it with the inspired Word of God. Though God speaks and prophetically reveals Himself and His will, it is possible to become sacrilegious, and lose focus of our dependence on God.

The Scripture gives several things to guard against creeping into our lives as we live for God. These negative actions are associated with the Holy Spirit and His work. They are the following:

> 1. Don't grieve the Spirit – This is when a person rejects the Holy Spirit and His work in their life especially when it comes to character development. (Ephesians 4:30)
> 2. Don't quench the Spirit – When the Holy Spirit is pushed away from

our lives, we become less sensitive to the things of God and the Spirit's voice. The fire of the Spirit begins to be extinguished. (I Thess. 5:19)

3. Don't rebel against the Spirit – To rebel against the Holy Spirit is to have a hardened heart in the midst of God's blessings. Israel is a great example of this in their wilderness wanderings. (Isaiah 63:10; Acts 7:51; Hebrews 3:15)

To avoid the above mentioned dangers, it is important to remember that the Holy Spirit is God. He must be revered with supreme devotion. Let us never become overly familiar with the work of the Holy Spirit, and lose the hunger and thirst for more of His presence in our lives.

Reflection: Is your walk with the Holy Spirit fresh and real in your life? What needs to be deleted or added to your life to make room for the Holy Spirit?

Day 46

The Holy Spirit and Renewal
I Timothy 4:1

It is important that we give heed to what is being said when the Holy Spirit has something to say. He has warned that in the last days there will be a great falling away from the faith. Please note that the Holy Spirit did not say there will be a lack of religion. Man has always had religion. Staying faithful to God and His word requires more than religion. It requires a relationship.

When Paul wrote to his son in the faith, Timothy, he encouraged him to not neglect the discipline of his faith. Timothy was encouraged to make sure maturity and progress was made. If he did pursue his walk with God, then he and those that followed would be saved. (I Timothy 4:15-16)

For Timothy the work of the Holy Spirit was important in life. He had been commissioned into the ministry when the hands of the presbytery were placed upon him with impartation of spiritual gifts, and a prophetic word from God. Even though he was propelled into his calling, Paul encouraged Timothy to not neglect the call and passion that came with it. (I Timothy 4:14) Later in Paul's last letter to Timothy, he also encouraged him to keep the gift of God stirred up and active with the fire of the Holy Spirit.

There have been many who have begun their journey with God filled with the fire of the Spirit to later burn out. It is easy to slip away from the simplicity of serving Christ into a religious lifestyle that doesn't involve the work of the Holy Spirit. To counteract this, a person must always be seeking the renewal of the Spirit in personal revival. It is then that the embers of the past are rekindled as the wind of the Spirit once again brings the fire of passion for the things of God.

Reflection: Pray for a personal revival in your life by allowing the Holy Spirit to rekindle in you a passion for God. Are you desperate for the manifested presence of God in your life?

Day 47

The Spirit of Grace
Hebrews 10:29

When God withholds from us what we deserve, we receive mercy. When God gives to us what we don't deserve, we receive grace. Because of sin, we all deserve eternal separation from the presence of God. Thankfully, we have salvation because God extended His grace toward us in Christ Jesus. The Holy Spirit is involved in every aspect of our salvation, and is known as the Spirit of Grace.

The title, "Spirit of Grace "is seldom mentioned in the Scripture, but holds deep meaning. The term is also found in Zech. 12:10 where the end of the great tribulation is pictured. A Jewish remnant is shown receiving a revelation of the true Messiah through the Spirit of Grace resulting in grief and emotional repentance.

The Spirit of Grace is God giving to us the richness of His goodness. This goodness is a revelation of God, especially for those that are not believers, leading them to repentance. To reject the goodness of God is to also reject the Spirit of Grace. (Romans 2:4)

For those that know Christ, there is a never ending supply of the goodness of God through the Spirit of Grace. How much of God's grace we need depends on how much we desire of God. The Apostle Paul needed a persistent trial removed from His life. When He sought the Lord, instead of the trial being removed, God granted him more grace to endure it. His weakness became an occasion for the Spirit of Grace. (II Cor. 12:7-10)

The Spirit of Grace is really the power of God at work in our lives as we rely less on ourselves, and more on Him. The frailty of who we are becomes the opportunity for God's power to be released.

Reflection: We have the promise that God will not withhold anything from us if we walk righteously before Him. (Psalm 84:11). Make seeking for more of God a priority in your life today.

Day 48

The Holy Spirit and the Antichrist
I John 4:1-3

Without a doubt we are living in the end time. The signs predicted in the Scriptures, and the events of the world show that the rise of a one world government and of a one world ruler is drawing closer.

The Holy Spirit has plenty to say about the end times. It was through the inspiration of the Holy Spirit that the prophets of old wrote and predicted what was revealed to them. (II Peter 1:19-21) And it will be through heeding the Word of God, and the work of the Holy Spirit in our lives that we will not be deceived by the spirit of the antichrist.

The spirit of deception is what governs the mindset of the world. The apostle Paul has instructed believers to constantly be aware of deceptive doctrines during the last days. (II Thess. 2:3). He also said that deception comes when there is no love for the truth. (II Thess. 2:10) If that is the case, the way to avoid the pitfalls of deception is to have an extreme love for the truth.

For those that truly have the Holy Spirit in their life, their greatest desire is to love and serve Jesus Christ. Their greatest proclamation is that

Jesus Christ is the Lord and Savior. This is what the world hates the most. The world will accept many religious proclamations, but it will never declare that Jesus Christ has come in the flesh as a man, and is at the same time God. The world is dominated by the spirit of the antichrist. Nevertheless, the day will come when every knee will bow before Christ, and proclaim Him Lord. (Philippians. 2:10-11)

For those that are children of God with the Holy Spirit in their life, they not only proclaim Jesus as the God/Man, but also have victory over the antichrist spirit of the world. (I John 4:4)

Reflection: The spirit of antichrist works through the spirit of fear. Identify the fears in your life, and with Holy Spirit authority rebuke the work of the enemy.

Day 49

"Yes," says the Holy Spirit.
Revelation 14:13

Even though many don't feel they can understand the Book of Revelation, it is important that it be a regular part of devotional study. The book is filled with many blessings including one for those that read and study it. (Rev. 1:3) It was not written to simply reveal future events, but as a revelation of Jesus Christ. (Rev. 1:1) Since the work of the Holy Spirit is to reveal Christ, the Spirit is found to be an integral part of it.

The writer is the Apostle John. From the beginning, he is overwhelmed by the presence of the Holy Spirit, and placed in a position where he is able to see into the future. Through the Holy Spirit, he was able to see events from the perspective of Heaven, Earth, and Hell.

At the beginning of the Revelation, the Holy Spirit addresses seven churches situated throughout the Asia Minor area. Each church received a commendation, and except for one, also received a warning. As each church received a word from the Holy Spirit they are cautioned to have an ear to listen intently to what He said. (Rev. 2-3)

As the events of the tribulation period are unfolded, a remnant is revealed that refuses to bow to the demands of the antichrist. They are persecuted and face martyrdom, but their reward is resting in the presence of the Lord away from the trials of this life.

The Holy Spirit is aware of the trials and tribulations we face. He instructs us, helps us, prays for us, and empowers us to be overcomers. The key is for us to remain faithful and patient in our Christian walk. If we do, there awaits for us the reward of eternal rest in the presence of the Lord. And to this the Holy Spirit says, "Yes." (Rev. 14:13)

Reflection: The final reference to the Holy Spirit in Scripture is an invitation to come and taste of the wonderful things He has for you. (Rev. 22:17) Be hungry and thirsty for the Holy Spirit, and you will be filled to overflowing.

Day 50

Have You Received Since You Believed?
(Acts 2:4; 10:46, 19:2)

In the verses listed above, record is given of individuals receiving the Baptism of the Holy Spirit. In each instance, Jesus was accepted as their Lord, and then afterward, as a separate experience, they were filled with the Holy Spirit and spoke in other tongues. Being filled with the Holy Spirit was the norm for the early church believer, and is available for us today.

Prayer is a constant in relation to being filled with the Holy Spirit. The days leading up to the Day of Pentecost were filled with continual devotion to prayer. (Acts 1:14) Later in Acts, fervent prayer preceded being once again filled with the Spirit. (Acts 4:31)

An important part of prayer is learning to wait. This was the instruction of Jesus to the disciples before the Holy Spirit was given to them. (Luke 24:49) At times, God wants us to wait before Him so He can prepare our lives to receive the gift of the Spirit.

Everything we receive from God is by His grace through faith. (Ephesians 2:8) The Holy

Spirit is a gift from the Heavenly Father and must be received by faith. (Galatians 3:1-3) Faith propels us to desire more of Jesus and His righteousness. For those who are hungry, He has promised they will be filled. (Luke 11:13)

The Bible doesn't record a set way of receiving the Holy Spirit. It shows hands being laid on individuals, while for others they received while in prayer, or hearing the message of the gospel.

If you have received Jesus as your Lord and Savior, begin by faith to earnestly and sincerely desire to be empowered by the Holy Spirit. By faith, receive the gift of the Holy Spirit, and let Him speak through you in a manner that magnifies and glorifies God. (Acts 2:11)

Dear Reader,

We sincerely hope the message in this book has encouraged you to accept the Salvation provided on the cross by our Lord Jesus Christ, or brought you into a deeper relationship with Him.

If you believe the message contained herein will benefit others, please help the author by recommending this book on your social media pages. Also, consider leaving a review on the retail site where this book was purchased.

If you would like to receive updates on future books by this author or publisher, please sign up for Empowered Publications Inc's newsletter at www.empoweredpublications.com.

Many blessings,

The Team at Empowered Publications Inc.